D1436844

Agatha Christie's
POIROT

THE ESSENTIAL NOVELS
IN ONE SITTING

by Jennifer Kasius

RUNNING PRESS
PHILADELPHIA · LONDON

9 8 7 6 5 4 3 2 1
Digit on the right indicates the number of this printing
Library of Congress Control Number: 2014937503
ISBN 978-0-7624-5460-0

Running Press Book Publishers
A Member of the Perseus Books Group
2300 Chestnut Street
Philadelphia, PA 19103-4371

Visit us on the web!
www.runningpress.com

❧ **Contents** ❧

❧ 3 ❧

AGATHA CHRISTIE, 1946

❧ Introduction ❧

AGATHA CHRISTIE is not only the best-selling *mystery* writer of all time, but also the best-selling *novelist*, ever. She follows only the Bible and Shakespeare in popularity, with worldwide sales of more than two billion copies to date. Christie was certainly industrious during her lifetime, writing more than eighty books (one for almost every year she lived). Her oeuvre expands beyond the mystery novel to include an autobiography, short story collections, popular plays (including *The Mousetrap* and *Witness for the Prosecution*), and even romances (written under the pseudonym Mary Westmacott).

But of course, it's the "who-dunit" for which we love her the most. It was evident from the time of Christie's first book, *The Mysterious Affair at Styles* (1920)—when her famous sleuth Hercule Poirot appears on the scene—that she knew the elements that make a good mystery. She recalls embarking on that first novel in her autobiography: "The whole point of a good detective story was that it must be somebody obvious, but at the same time . . . you would find that it was not obvious, that he could not possibly have done it. Though really of course, he *had* done it."

That's the "trick" she uses consistently throughout her work—always surprising her readers who feel quite sure they have it all figured out. Of course, she plants plenty of false clues and red herrings along the way, just to spice things up. And there are also the shocking plot twists—one of which, famously done in *The Murder of Roger Ackroyd*, caused quite a stir when published. Some of her detractors charged that she wasn't "playing fair." Yet in re-reading any Christie mystery, we know that she certainly *does* play fair. She gives her readers all the clues and hints they need—yet almost always, she manages to shock us in the end.

Christie confessed that when she first started writing mysteries, she was firmly entrenched in the Sherlock Holmes conceit. She provided an eccentric detective (Poirot), an assistant who acts as a foil (Captain Hastings), as well as an "insider" from Scotland Yard to help with investigations (Inspector Japp). At the time of *Styles* publication she was working at the dispensary during World War I, and had access to many poisons. It was her growing knowledge of various drugs and their reactions that inspired this first plot, and figured in many of her subsequent mysteries.

She would later insert many of her interests and passions in her novels, setting one novel aboard the Orient Express, for example. Christie was much enamored of train travel, and journeyed to Istanbul in 1928 on the famed railway, embarking on an exciting adventure as a new divorcee. After marrying her second husband, renowned archeologist Max Mallowan, she made several subsequent journeys to the Middle East, and often used it as a setting for her novels (including *Death On the Nile*, *Murder in Mesopotamia*, *Death*

Comes as the End, among others). She was also fond of writing the "closed estate" murder mystery—wherein all the suspects are enclosed in one remote location (as in *Ten Little Indians*, *4:50 from Paddington*, and many others). Her knowledge of English village life (and the villagers' love of gossip) figures in most of her work, particularly in the stories surrounding her beloved busybody sleuth, Miss Jane Marple.

But it is Poirot who "wins" upon examining Christie's entire body of work: He is the sleuth that she returns to most often, most likely because he was the detective that was most popular with her fans. She admits to eventually loathing her creation. Poirot's trademark pomposity and meticulous nature wore rather thin with her. But unlike Arthur Conan Doyle, who also came to dislike his sleuth, Christie did not kill him off in the height of his popularity. Instead, she took a precautionary measure of sorts by composing the novel *Curtain: Poirot's Last Case* during the London Blitz of the Second World War. In the event of her death, she wanted to give her fans a satisfying "end" to the beloved character. Of course, it turned out she did not die in the Blitz, but carried on for several more decades. *Curtain* was finally published in 1975, a few months before her own death. In the novel, Poirot is reunited with his dear friend Captain Hastings to solve a mystery at the estate where it all started—Styles Manor. It's a satisfying full-circle story arc, and proof that Agatha Christie cared for her fans. She wanted to send off her popular detective with a flourish.

The "Life" of Hercule Poirot

"It is the brain, the little grey cells, on which one must rely. One must seek the truth from within—not without."

— Poirot

H ercule Poirot was "born" in the novel *The Mysterious Affair at Styles*, in which he is a war refugee

Portrait of the fictional Belgian detective, Hercule Poirot, published in *The Sketch* in 1923

from Belgium living in a remote English village. He is a retired police officer famous in his own land for cracking difficult cases. Christie describes him as a small man, only five feet four inches, with an egg-shaped head and a rather prominent mustache. In her autobiography, Christie writes at length on how she conceived the character: "he would be meticulous, very tidy. I could see him . . . always arranging things, linking things in pairs, liking things square instead of round." (Modern readers can't help but wonder if the OCD character in *Monk* was partly based on Poirot.) She also determines that he would be brainy, and be reliant on his "little grey cells" (a recurring phrase from Poirot). He should also have a grand yet quirky name, just like Sherlock Holmes.

Poirot has other similarities to Holmes, relying on order and method to solve crimes. He also has an overblown ego, saying without irony in one novel that he is "the finest brain in Europe." Unlike Holmes, it is primarily Poirot's knowledge of human nature that leads him to crack many cases—from the personality profiles he gathers in *Cards on the Table*, to his chilling perception that all human beings have the capability to murder in *Death on the Nile*. In *Curtain*, he proves this theory to be true even to his own character (more to be revealed later).

Throughout many of the novels, Poirot cracks cases with his friend, Captain Arthur Hastings (who takes a similar role to the often-obtuse Watson) and Inspector Japp, a professional connection much in the tradition of Holmes' Scotland Yarder, Lestrade. But Poirot also has help from others, including the eccentric mystery novelist, Mrs. Ariadne Oliver (based on Christie herself); his organized secretary, Miss Felicity

Lemon; and secret service agent
Colonel Race. Throughout the
decades of Poirot mysteries, we see
him go from a war refugee to a
failed attempt at growing vegetable marrows in a sleepy village to
finally settling at the Whitehaven
Mansions in London (the art-
deco architecture being perfectly
symmetrical, of course). His friend
Hastings goes from bachelor
to husband to South American
rancher, and finally to a widower

returning to England in the final
novel, *Curtain*. Though Poirot had
consistently gently chided Hastings for his general inability to use
his own "little grey cells"—their
friendship lasted a half-century. Of
course, sticklers for chronology
will be glad to know that Christie realized her error, "I saw what
a terrible mistake I had made in
starting with Hercule Poirot so
old." But at the time she conceived him in 1920, could she

have imagined that she would still be writing Poirot stories through five decades?

Poirot was so beloved by Christie fans, it seemed a challenge to actors to fit in his shoes on the big screen, but many great actors have taken on the task: Albert Finney received an Academy Award for his role in *Murder on the Orient Express* in 1974. Peter Ustinov reprised the role in six movies, including *Death on the*

ALBERT FINNEY, 1974

PETER USTINOV, 1982

Nile and *Evil Under the Sun*. Christie's daughter Rosalind famously remarked "That's not Poirot!" referring to Ustinov not being true to her mother's vision of the detective. Without missing a beat, the actor notoriously quipped, "He is now!"

Probably the most famous (and accurate) Poirot portrayal has been by David Suchet, who played the famous detective for almost a quarter-century, in made-for-TV movies from 1989 to 2013. Suchet admits in interviews to always reviewing Christie's novels to ensure that he is channeling her character properly—and most Poirot fans agree he's done a wonderful job of it!

Christie's writing abilities faded in her later years, so the year before she died she unvaulted the final Poirot novel, which she had written decades earlier. At the time of *Curtain*'s publication in 1975, (where the sleuth meets his

DAVID SUCHET, 1995

demise) Poirot was the only fictional character to have received a front-page obituary in the *New York Times*. Imagine, a sleuth occupying the same print space usually only afforded to world leaders! Poirot is a detective whose popularity has endured now for nearly a century—he is indeed a little man who remains large in the hearts and minds of mystery fans.

Warning to Readers

The following little book summarizes the "best" of the Poirot novels—nine of the most famous and beloved mysteries. SPOILER ALERT: the culprit is revealed in each of the summaries. This tiny tome can be used in many ways: as a means of revisiting the mysteries

you already love; to read afresh if
you really don't mind the "twist"
ending getting spoiled or the cul-
prits revealed; or perhaps you may
want to read these plot summaries
AFTER you've viewed a Poirot
movie and are left wondering,
"Wait, why did so-and-so do that?
How was he/she related?" Never
fear—these summaries are true
accounts of Christie's original plots.
You may see them adapted and "tampered with" when viewing some of

the screen interpretations—but this
little guide will help ground you
in what Christie actually wrote,
and how she originally presented
her masterful plots. So settle into a
comfortable armchair by the fire.
As Poirot would do, you may pour
some wine (in perfectly symmetrical glasses) to sip on while enjoying
these little mysteries. Your "little
grey cells" will thank you!

The Mysterious Affair at Styles

(1920)

"Imagination is a good servant, and a bad master. The simplest explanation is always the most likely."

—Poirot

❧ MAIN CHARACTERS ❧

JOHN CAVENDISH: *Hastings' old friend and presumed heir of the Styles Estate*

MARY CAVENDISH: *John's reserved yet alluring wife*

LAWRENCE CAVENDISH: *John's brother, a dilettante with a head for medicine and a heart for poetry*

EMILY CAVENDISH INGLETHORPE: *the formidable matriarch of the Styles household*

ALFRED INGLETHORPE: *Emily's much younger husband*

CYNTHIA MURDOCH: *Emily's ward and a worker at the dispensary, with much knowledge of poisons*

EVELYN "EVIE" HOWARD: *Emily's companion, a no-nonsense woman who speaks her mind*

DORCAS: *the parlormaid*

MRS. RAIKES: *a notorious temptress in town*

The story takes place in 1916, when Arthur Hastings is at a convalescent home recovering from a war wound. He runs into an old acquaintance, John Cavendish, who invites him to his family's home for a restful recovery. Styles Manor is an old country house, stately and isolated, located two miles from the tiny village of Styles St. Mary. Hastings remembers John's mother from when he was a child. Emily Cavendish had been a fortysomething woman when she married John's father. Now, decades older, she is in possession of the Cavendish fortune, and it's clear that she definitely runs the show. She controls the financial fates not only of her two stepsons (who call her "The Mater") but also of her ward, Cynthia Murdoch; her companion, Evelyn "Evie" Howard; and her new husband, Alfred Ingelthorpe. Emily's recent marriage has raised some eyebrows—Alfred is twenty years her junior, and odd in appearance and demeanor. John calls him "a rotten little bounder," and the family generally tolerates him, even though they assume he's a gold-digger. Hastings' impression is that Alfred is definitely an odd bird, but he *does* he seem devoted to his new wife.

Emily proudly states to Hastings that they a war household, and nothing goes to waste at Styles, "every scrap of waste paper, even."

While the Cavendish brothers lead a life of idle entitlement, the young women at Styles contribute to the war effort: Cynthia works at a dispensary, and John's wife, Mary, works the land, rising early in the morning to tend the fields.

During Hastings' stay, there is a bit of a scene: Evie is suddenly banished from the estate after speaking her mind about Alfred. "He'd sooner murder you in your bed!" she warns Emily. . . She also hints that Alfred is spending some time with the fetching young widow in town, Mrs. Raikes.

Meanwhile, Hastings gets a wonderful surprise while exploring the village—he is reunited with an old friend, Hercule Poirot! Once one of the most celebrated members of the Belgian police, Poirot is now a war refugee. He and his Belgian compatriots have come to Styles St. Mary because of the kindness of Emily Inglethorpe. She has funded their passage to England, and he owes her a great debt.

Hastings returns to the estate that afternoon, and hears that another brouhaha has occurred: Emily presumably had a huge row with her husband behind closed doors. The parlormaid Dorcas clearly heard her say, "You have lied to me, deceived me." Later Hastings overhears Mary having an argument with her mother-in-law. He hears Mary say, "I might have

DAVID SUCHET AS HERCULE POIROT,
IN *THE MYSTERIOUS AFFAIR AT STYLES* (TV)

known you would shield him." Dinner that evening is a strained affair—the air thick with tension. After dinner Alfred announces that he has an appointment with their accountant in town, and that he may be out late. Emily says she will retire early.

The household is awakened at 5 a.m. by Emily's tortured cries. She's clearly in distress, but her bedroom doors have been bolted and no one can reach her. Hastings and Lawrence are able to break down her door, but it's too late: Emily has one last horrible convulsion and dies. The doctor strongly suspects strychnine poisoning. Lawrence passionately, though illogically, claims that his stepmother must have died from natural causes. But anyone who witnessed her last moments knows that she must have been poisoned. Lawrence should know that as well as anyone, since he went to medical school. Why would he so passionately deny that his stepmother was poisoned? The only member of the household not present for Emily's demise is her husband: he had been detained at the accountant's house, and spent the night there rather than returning home.

Poirot is called in to investigate unofficially, as he will do so with the utmost discretion. Plus, he owes it to his benefactress to find out who murdered her.

When Poirot examines Emily's bedroom, he is struck by many intriguing clues, among them a locked document case; a still-wet coffee stain on the floor; a fragment of dark green fabric in the door latch; and spilled candle wax on the floor.

Dorcas states that her mistress always had a cup of cocoa in the middle of the night. But no traces of strychnine were found in the cocoa. Was it in the coffee Emily had after dinner? No, it couldn't be, because the effects from the poison started at 5 a.m.—several hours after she ingested the coffee.

There are more puzzling facts: Why did Emily order a fire in her room in the middle of July? Traces of a burned will are found in the grate. She had just drawn up a new will that afternoon, and had the servants witness her signature. Why would she write and destroy a will the very day of her death?

Dorcas also notes that her mistress seemed very distressed that afternoon, saying to her, "Never trust a man, they aren't worth it." Lastly, another curious occurrence . . . Emily's document case has been tampered with. It must have held something incriminating.

At the inquest, the town chemist testifies that Alfred bought strychnine the day before the murder, allegedly to poison a dog. When Alfred takes the stand, he calmly states that he did not buy the strychnine. But when asked his whereabouts at the time the strychnine is purchased, he remains silent. Why doesn't he defend himself? It almost seems like Alfred *wants* to get arrested!

And according to Inspector Japp, that's exactly what is likely to happen: He thinks it's an open-and-shut case. But for Poirot, it's a little too simple. What kind of man would so obviously buy strychnine

the day before he murders his wife?
Poirot suspects someone impersonated Alfred—after all, the man has
a very distinct "look" that would
be easy to duplicate—with a black
beard and gold pince-nez. Dorcas
remembers that there's a "dress-up"
box in the attic. Sure enough, they
discover a fake black beard!

Another one of Poirot's hunches
proves true: The day Alfred supposedly bought the strychnine, he was
actually escorting Mrs. Raikes in

the village. Poirot exposes Alfred's alibi, thus clearing Alfred from suspicion. Evie is outraged. She is fierce in her hatred of him, and will not be swayed in her belief that he is the murderer.

Meanwhile, Hastings has become quite the "Father Confessor." The beautiful Mary Cavendish admits to Hastings that she isn't happy in her marriage. But it seems like she's holding something back—what is she hiding? Cynthia then unburdens herself, saying how distressed she is that Emily hadn't provided for her in her will. As a penniless orphan, what will she do? Hastings then attempts a very awkward marriage proposal, which seems just the thing to lighten Cynthia's mood. After she rejects him with a laugh, a befuddled Hastings is left with his pride a bit wounded. But he soldiers on, and continues to help Poirot with the case.

Soon after, John Cavendish is arrested for the murder of his step-mother. Both the gold pince-nez and the strychnine were found among his belongings, and it seems he made a sloppy attempt to forge Alfred's signature when he bought the poison. Poirot looks conflicted about something, but then states cryptically to Hastings that he has decided to risk something for a woman's happiness.

Poirot is frustrated that he can't find the "last link" that would crack the case. Aha! Suddenly it is all clear in Poirot's mind. He gathers everyone together to explain:

Emily was not quarreling with Alfred that afternoon; rather, it was with her stepson, John. He was the one who was carrying on the dalliance with Mrs. Raikes. That afternoon, Emily was admonishing John for disgracing the family, and firmly told him to break off the affair. Mary Cavendish, a jealous woman, thought that her mother-in-law had evidence of John's affair, and was protecting him. But it was quite the contrary: Emily was planning on disinheriting her stepson that very afternoon, based on his behavior. She hastily made out a will to clearly state that her husband would inherit the estate and the money, and had her servants witness it. She went to get stamps so she could send it promptly to her solicitor and found she didn't

have any, so she went looking in
her husband's desk, where she
discovered an incriminating letter,
that said, *"My dearest Evelyn . . .
There's a good time coming once the
old woman is out of the way."*

Alfred's and Evie's apparent
loathing of one another was all a
ruse! Utterly shocked at her husband's treachery, Emily hides the
incriminating letter in her document case, then burns her new will,
leaving traces in the grate. She knew

she was in some form of danger, but not sure exactly how.

She couldn't have foreseen that her husband had simply mixed her regular medicine with bromide powders. The bromide would cause the medicine's trace amounts of strychnine to concentrate in the last dose. Alfred would be the most obvious suspect, so he and his lover Evie devised an elaborate plan to clear him of the crime and frame John. While

Alfred was very clearly establishing an alibi by being seen with Mrs. Raikes, Evie disguised herself as Alfred and bought strychnine from the chemist. Evie has a brawny build, so with a fake beard and glasses, she made a convincing "Alfred." She signs for the poison by mimicking John's handwriting, and later plants the disguise among John's belongings. It works like a charm, Alfred is accused then cleared, and John is arrested.

Except for the glitch of Emily discovering Alfred's letter, it almost worked perfectly. . .

Soon after Emily's death, Alfred knows that his wife must have discovered his letter and locked it in the document case in her bedroom. But the crime scene is closed off! Desperate, he sneaks into the bedroom and breaks the lock. But where to put the letter? It can't be found on his person (and he can't throw it away, as every scrap of paper is saved in the war household). A fire in July would be suspicious. So the only thing he can do is tear the paper in three strips, and hide them in the three vases on the bedroom mantelpiece. The "last link" was under Poirot's nose at the crime scene the whole time. Being very sensitive to disorder, Poirot had suddenly remembered that the vases had been moved slightly since his first visit to the crime scene. *Voila!* The damning evidence!

How are the other strange clues explained? Mary had sneaked into her mother-in-law's bed-room that fateful night. Mad with jealousy, she was looking for the "evidence" that would prove her husband's infidelity. As she was skulking about, Emily began her fatal convulsions. Scared, shocked, and panicked, Mary spills the coffee, her candle, and then runs out of the room, leaving behind a trace of fabric on the door latch. The strange clues at the crime scene are explained.

Poirot knew that John wasn't guilty the whole time he was incarcerated. But he suspected that John's troubles would awaken his wife's dormant love for him, so he let him spend some time in jail. Mary is now newly devoted to her husband. It also turns out that Lawrence was secretly love with Cynthia, but was worried she may have committed the crime—hence his strange insistence that his step-mother died of natural causes.

Love and peace are now restored to Styles Manor, and Hasting and Poirot have solved their first case together!

The Murder of Roger Ackroyd

(1926)

"Everything is simple, if you arrange the facts methodically."

—Poirot

◆ MAIN CHARACTERS ◆

DR. JAMES SHEPPARD: *the village doctor of King's Abbot*

CAROLINE SHEPPARD: *his sister, whose favorite pastime is knowing everyone's business*

ROGER ACKROYD: *a successful business tycoon*

MRS. FERRARS: *a widow and presumed soon-to-be Mrs. Roger Ackroyd*

FLORA: *Ackroyd's niece*

RALPH PATON: *Ackroyd's stepson*

PARKER: *the butler*

MRS. RUSSELL: *the housekeeper*

URSULA BOURNE: *the parlormaid*

GEOFFREY RAYMOND: *Ackroyd's
    secretary*

The Murder of Roger Ackroyd is considered one of the best detective stories of all time, chiefly because of its brilliant surprise ending. Dr. James Sheppard is the narrator of this particular tale. Hastings is absent from this story, so Dr. Sheppard fills that role of Poirot's right-hand man, witnessing the detective's calm reasoning in cracking the case.

Dr. Sheppard is a mild-mannered doctor in the small village

of King's Abbot. His sister Caroline is the chief gossiper in town, and seems to know of everyone's comings-and-goings—as well as all the rumors. When Dr. Sheppard's patient, the widow Mrs. Ferrars, is found dead from an overdose of verdanol, the rumor is that she took her own life. But why would she do such a thing? It was largely understood that she and Ackroyd would be getting married soon. Roger Ackroyd is a widower, a rich businessman, and very much the main benefactor of the King's Abbot community. He lives in a monstrosity of an estate called Fernly Park, along with his deceased brother's wife and her daughter, Flora, both of whom are very dependent on him for money.

Since Mrs. Ferrars' husband died a year ago, she and Ackroyd had been growing closer, having an unfortunate history in common: Both had been married to miserable drunks. Ackroyd's first wife had died of the bottle many years before, and after her death Ackroyd has been good enough to raise her son, Ralph Paton, as his own.

Dr. Sheppard is a good friend of Ackroyd's, and soon he is taken into his confidence one evening after dinner. Ackroyd is very much troubled: The day before she died, Mrs. Ferrars had confessed that she had poisoned her abusive husband. Ackroyd admits to Sheppard that he was shocked when he heard his fiancée's admission of guilt. Mrs. Ferrars went on to say that only *one* other person knew of her crime, and had been blackmailing her for large sums of money. She didn't reveal the identity of her blackmailer, but Ackroyd vowed that he will find out. He charges that the blackmailing scoundrel "drove her to death as surely as if he'd killed her." The evening post arrives, and with it a letter from Mrs. Ferrars

writing from "beyond the grave"—
presumably to reveal the identity
of her blackmailer. Dr. Sheppard is
on the edge of his seat as Ackroyd
opens the letter, but suddenly Ackroyd thinks the better of it and says
he wants to finish reading the letter
in private. Thus dismissed, the good
doctor leaves Ackroyd's study at ten
minutes to nine o'clock.

Later that night, Sheppard gets
a telephone call summoning him
back to Fernly Park. Ackroyd has

been murdered! When Sheppard arrives, the butler, Parker, is surprised and denies making the call. Ackroyd's study is locked, so they break down the door and find the victim stabbed in the neck. Sheppard instructs Parker to phone the police immediately. He is also careful to report that he did what little had to be done at the crime scene, and did not disturb the position of the body. He observes the room: The door has been bolted from the inside and the window is open, with muddy footprints on the window ledge. It's clear that the culprit must have entered through the window. But who could it be?

Once the inspector arrives, the various members of Fernly Park are questioned. Ackroyd's secretary, Geoffrey Raymond, reports that his employer had been very much alive at nine-thirty. He's sure because he had passed by the study door and overheard Ackroyd speaking to someone. He distinctly remembers that Ackroyd said, "*the calls upon my purse have been so frequent of late that I fear it is impossible for me to accede to your request.*" A very strange thing to say—but could he have been face-to-face with the blackmailer? Flora Ackroyd tells the police that she saw her uncle at a quarter to ten, when she went to bid him goodnight and he told her he didn't want to be disturbed. So the time of death must have been from

9:45 to 10:15, when Sheppard got the telephone call. So who does *not* have an alibi for that time period?

Turns out, several of the inhabitants of Fernly Park seem a bit fishy upon investigation. Parker had blackmailed his former employer before working for Ackroyd. There is something suspicious about the new parlormaid, Ursula Bourne. There are also reports that a mysterious stranger was lurking in the bushes that night. But of all these suspects, the most likely culprit is Ralph Paton. Several strikes are against him: for one, he has disappeared, and has not been seen since the murder. Two, according to Ackroyd's will, most of his fortune and estate is bequeathed to his stepson. What's more, the footprints on the ledge have been traced to a pair of shoes that Ralph owns. Things are not looking good for Ralph!

Enter Hercule Poirot. He has retired to King's Abbot in an

unsuccessful attempt to tend a garden and raise vegetable marrows. Flora Ackroyd knows of Poirot's reputation, and implores him to get involved. Flora and Ralph had been secretly engaged. Ackroyd was very keen on the match, and had planned on announcing their nuptials soon. Flora doesn't seem that passionate about Ralph, but seems duty-bound to clear his name. And she is certain that Ralph wouldn't have had the gumption to murder his stepfather—he is as spineless as the rest of the family, who depended on Ackroyd to keep them in comfort.

Flora admits that there was a general resentment toward Ackroyd for keeping a close watch on the purse strings. Though Ackroyd was very generous to the general community, he tended to be miserly with his nearest and dearest, which drove her to steal forty pounds from her uncle's bedroom. She was almost caught in the act by Parker, but in a wave of quick thinking she had pretended to come out of Ackroyd's study. She remorsefully admits that she never actually saw her uncle alive at 9:45. So that changes the possible time of death—to just after 9:30, when Raymond had over-heard Ackroyd's voice in the study.

More curious clues surface: a piece of torn cloth found in the summerhouse, a quill pen with traces of heroin in it, a wedding ring found at the bottom of the pond with the inscription, "*From R., March 13th.*" Could Roger Ackroyd and Mrs. Ferrars have secretly eloped? Or is Ralph already married to Flora? And there's more about Ursula Bourne: The day he died, Ackroyd had abruptly fired her for disturbing papers on his desk. What did she see? Also, who made the fake telephone call to Sheppard on that fateful evening? And where did Ralph Paton disappear to, and why?

The answers to these questions are eventually revealed by Poirot. Sheppard accompanies him through all the sleuthing and gives an accurate report on their findings. Many things puzzle Sheppard, but all the while, Poirot's wheels are turning. Poirot often cryptically proclaims, "You cannot hide much from Hercule Poirot!" and "Poirot will soon know everything!"

Poirot gathers all the suspects together and reveals his discoveries: First, the identity of the mysterious stranger is the long-lost illegitimate, drug-addicted son of Mrs. Russell. Mother and son met under cloak of night at the summerhouse, where he tried to bilk his estranged mother of more money to feed his habit.

The second red herring: Ursula Bourne has been secretly wed to Ralph Paton—since March 13th, as the lost wedding ring indicates. Ackroyd had been very keen to marry his niece to Ralph, and had no idea that Ralph married the maid instead. Ralph had been working up the courage to tell his uncle the truth, but soon acted in predictable spineless fashion. In a fit of angry frustration, Ursula told Ackroyd herself. Upon hearing the news, Ackroyd flew into a temper and fired her. Later that fateful night, she met her husband in the summerhouse, and Ralph scolded her for endangering his inheritance. In a rage, she flung her wedding ring into the pond and tore her apron on a nail in a dramatic departure.

When Ackroyd is murdered later that night, things look bad for Ursula, as she doesn't have an alibi for the time of the murder. It would be unthinkable for Ralph to have to give testimony that would incriminate his wife, so his only option is to run away. But who convinced him to disappear? And who provided sanctuary? It was none other than Sheppard—who conveniently left that fact out of his account. He knew of an asylum Ralph could escape to and not be found. Sheppard explains he was just acting out of concern for Ralph's best interests.

What else did Sheppard leave out of his narrative? Something very important. . . he is the murderer of Roger Ackroyd! He is also the blackmailer of Mrs. Ferrars!

Upon re-reading his account of the case, the reader sees that he has faithfully reported the truth, just not the *whole* truth. He has omitted key things. For example, when he left Ackroyd's study, he writes "*It was just on ten minutes to nine when I left him, the letter still unread. I hesitated with my hand on the door handle, looking back and wondering if there was anything I had left undone.*" But what he doesn't say is that he stabbed Ackroyd in the neck, then bolted the study door from the inside and opened the window. He had taken a pair of Ralph's shoes and made the print on the ledge. Then he set up Ackroyd's dictaphone to go off at exactly half-past nine, thus making it seem as if Ackroyd was still alive. He arranged for a patient to make a call to his house under false pretenses—so that his sister would witness his summons to Fernly Park. He needed to be first on the crime scene in order to get rid of the dictaphone. As Parker was calling the police, Sheppard had ample time to slip the dictaphone into his doctor's bag and nonchalantly carry it away.

But why would an otherwise gentle man do such a thing? He had darkness lurking in him all along. When the opportunity for blackmail presented itself, he couldn't resist. As a doctor, he knew that Mrs. Ferrars' husband had not died of natural causes, but rather of poisoning. This was a once-in-a-lifetime opportunity— he was always tending to the rich, but was never able to get ahead in his role of the meek country doctor. Greed and resentment got the best of him. But now that Poirot knows all, Sheppard's only concern is to save his sister from grief and embarrassment. He takes the same drug, veranol, that killed Mrs. Ferrars. In the final chapter, titled "Apologia," he writes. "*I have no pity for myself . . . But I wish Hercule Poirot had never retired from work and come here to grow vegetable marrows."*

Peril at End House

(1932)

"You have a tendency, Hastings, to prefer the least likely. That, no doubt, is from reading too many detective stories."

—Poirot

MAIN CHARACTERS

MAGDALA "NICK" BUCKLEY: *a bubbly socialite and owner of the dilapidated estate of End House*

FREDERICA "FREDDIE" RICE: *her best friend*

CHARLES VYSE: *Nick's solicitor, who also happens to be her cousin*

GEORGE CHALLENGER & JIM LAZARUS: *two suitors who hang about End House*

MAGGIE BUCKLEY: *Nick's shy cousin from Yorkshire*

MICHAEL SETON: *an aviator and adventurer, recently deceased*

MR. AND MRS. CROFT: *a nice couple from Australia*

Hercule Poirot is on holiday at a resort in Cornwall, along with his traveling companion, Captain Hastings. There, he meets Nick Buckley, the sole owner of the neighboring estate, End House. Nick is an unusual name for a young woman, (it was her grandfather's moniker) but she explains that she was christened Magdala—as it's a name that has been passed down in her family for generations.

Nick seems flighty and frivolous, and downright blasé about her recent brushes with death. She laughs about the things that she reports to Poirot: The brakes have given out in her car, a heavy picture fell over her bed, and a boulder narrowly missed her while she was out strolling. Nick is amused by it all, but Poirot is dead serious. He's all the more concerned when Nick waves a wasp away from her head—and finds that it was not a wasp, but rather a bullet that has flown through her floppy hat! Poirot agrees to take her under his wing and investigate who could be making these attempts on her life.

He discovers a bit more about Nick and those closest to her: Nick is an orphan who has inherited the crumbling mansion of End House. Nick reports that the dear old place is mortgaged to the hilt, and that she doesn't have a penny to her name to fix her family home. She receives rent from an Australian couple who live in the lodge on the grounds, a Mr. and Mrs. Croft. There's also her best friend, Frederica Rice, and a couple of suitors who hang around the place: Art dealer Jim Lazarus and George Challenger. Nick's closest living relation is her cousin Charles Vyse, a lawyer in the nearby village of St. Loo.

As he makes his rounds with questioning, Poirot finds that

Mrs. Croft is an invalid, while Mr. Croft is a doting husband. But Poirot wonders if they are really as harmless as they seem. Their demeanors seem exaggerated, almost like they are deliberately acting like a doddering, elderly couple. And then there's Frederica, or "Freddie," a fragile-looking girl who seems rather haunted about something. Poirot hears that she was abused by her husband, and is trying to get a divorce. She's also fighting a nasty addiction to cocaine. Then there's Charles, an uptight man of the law. Charles tells Poirot that his cousin is passionately devoted to her family home—but this characterization of Nick seems to run counter to her happy-go-lucky demeanor.

Upon Poirot's request, Nick sends for her cousin Maggie, who comes down from Yorkshire right away. Poirot thinks that a companion may help to protect Nick from further danger. Maggie turns out to be a rather unassuming girl, the daughter of a vicar. Her simple and unsophisticated manner seems to be quite a contrast to the flamboyant and gregarious Nick.

There's a big party that night, and Nick looks resplendent in a black frock with a very distinctive red Chinese shawl upon her shoulders. While everyone is out marveling at the fireworks display, Maggie announces that she's going inside to fetch her coat. Soon, there is a huddled figure in the corner—it's a woman, shot dead. She's wearing a Chinese shawl! It's assumed that it's Nick, but it turns out to be Maggie. Poirot chastises himself for his stupidity—he wasn't able to find the culprit in time, and now a lethal blow has been struck! The bullet was clearly meant for Nick—but who could it be?

Meanwhile, the newspapers report that Michael Seton, the

renowned pilot who had recently gone missing while making a trip across the globe, is confirmed dead. Just before he died, Michael had inherited a huge fortune from his uncle. Nick seems absolutely inconsolable over the news of Seton's death, and it's soon revealed why: Michael and Nick had been secretly engaged, and she produces his love letters to prove it. What's more, Michael has just willed his fortune to his fiancée,

Magdala Buckley. She is now a very rich woman!

The plot certainly thickens— Poirot asks if Nick has ever made a last will and testament. Nick, in scatterbrained fashion, recalls writing one a few months ago, when she about to have surgery for appendicitis. But she can't find it—wait, now she remembers . . . after it was witnessed and signed, Nick had asked Mr. Croft to post it to her lawyer/cousin Charles. But Charles denies having ever received it, while Mr. Croft swears to sending it. Who is telling the truth? Back when Nick had written it, it had hardly mattered who got her money, because she had been poor as a church mouse. She had simply left the little she had to Freddie. Hmmm . . . But now that Nick is a very rich woman, this missing will is all the more important.

Poirot affirms that Nick is in dire danger. He hides her away in a nursing home, with strict orders not to have any visitors. Even more importantly, he instructs, do NOT eat anything from the "outside." The murderer is loose, and will most assuredly strike again!

Nick ignores Poirot's orders and eats a chocolate—which turns out is laced with cocaine. Though she becomes violently sick, she'll pull through. Why, Poirot asks, did she go against his wishes? She explains that she thought the box of chocolates were okay to eat, since they were sent from Poirot himself. Alas, the murderer is brazen, going so far as to forge Poirot's name on the card! Freddie is immediately suspected, since she would have ready access to the drug.

The poisoned chocolates are the last straw for Poirot—it's time for extreme measures to catch the killer. He issues a false report that Nick has died. Sure enough, the missing will unexpectedly turns up.

Poirot says he will assemble everyone together to read Nick's last will and testament aloud. This will be a carefully orchestrated "play" sure to entrap the murderer.

A strange thing happens in the meantime: Poirot and Hastings are startled by a pale, cruel face staring at them from the window. The mysterious stranger just as suddenly disappears. Who could it be?

The time has come to put on the "play." Poirot reads Nick's will.

The bulk of her estate goes to none other than . . . Mrs. Croft!

Upon hearing the news, Mrs. Croft seems overjoyed but not at all surprised. She remains mysterious, saying only that she did something for Nick's father many years ago in Australia—thus making Nick forever indebted to her. Everyone is absolutely flabbergasted. To ease the shock, Poirot suggests a séance to call upon Nick's spirit. Nick (very much alive) appears as an apparition.

Mrs. Croft nearly faints from shock. She has been caught red-handed. Inspector Japp steps out of the shadows and affirms that Mrs. Croft is really Maggie Miller, a criminal wanted for forgery! Nick's forged will was a brilliant master stroke—something that almost made Mrs. Croft and her accomplice husband very rich indeed!

Suddenly a shot rings out. A bullet has grazed Freddie's shoulder. Then another body is found—it's the mysterious stranger, who turns out to be Freddie's estranged, drug-addicted husband. In his desperation to feed his habit, he tried to kill his wife, then turned the gun upon himself. But the dead man is not the murderer. No, Poirot now knows who is responsible for Maggie's death . . .

Mademoiselle Nick! The setup has been brilliant: Nick invented the threats to her life. She knew if she "just happened" to consult the brilliant detective Hercule Poirot, he would advise her to send for a friend for added protection: The perfect reason to have her cousin Maggie at End House. Maggie was the intended victim, not Nick! Maggie's name was also Magdala Buckley, and it was she who was engaged to Michael Seton, not Nick. How convenient that Nick shared the name with her cousin. She just had to get Maggie out of the way and pose as the sole Magdala Buckley to inherit the vast

Seton fortune. Nick was mad for money, and desperately in love with End House. She would do anything to save her beloved estate, even resort to murder! Nick had lent her cousin her shawl at the party, making it seem like Maggie's murder was a case of mistaken identity. In reality, Nick had taken a hidden pistol that she kept in a secret panel in the parlor, and shot Maggie dead.

Even Poirot was fooled, as he did everything in his power to protect the "damsel in distress," Nick. But she really was a heartless fiend, hoping that her will would point suspicion to her "best friend," Freddie. She even took her pistol and planted it among Freddie's belongings. As an added touch, Nick poisoned herself with cocaine, making it seem all the more convincing that the murderer was at large. But she was smart enough to take *just enough*, and not cause any serious damage. Now that she is caught, she asks for Freddie's wristwatch before she is taken into custody by Inspector Japp. A strange request, but both Poirot and Freddie know why she asked for the trinket. The watch contains a hidden stash of cocaine—a dose strong enough to kill. She will commit suicide in order to escape the gallows.

Freddie announces that she is recovering from her drug habit, and plans on marrying Jim Lazarus. Commander Challenger is revealed to be a drug dealer. And the Crofts are also brought to justice. Charles Vyse will inherit End House. Undoubtedly Poirot has been chastened (though his ego not exactly humbled), knowing he should not have been taken in by a young and pretty woman. Nick was very cunning, but in the end, not cunning enough to fool Hercule Poirot!

Murder on the Orient Express

(1934)

*"The impossible could not
have happened, therefore the
impossible must be possible in
spite of appearances."*

—Poirot

⤝ MAIN CHARACTERS ⤜

MONSIEUR BOUC: *director of the Wagon-Lit train company*

PIERRE MICHEL: *the train's conductor*

MARY DEBENHAM & COLONEL ARBUTHNOT: *two very proper Britishers*

RATCHETT: *a menacing-looking man, in fear for his life*

HECTOR MACQUEEN: *Rachett's assistant*

EDWARD MASTERMAN: *Ratchett's valet*

ANTONIO FOSCARELLI: *an Italian entrepreneur*

MRS. HUBBARD: *a walking stereotype of the "Ugly American Abroad"*

PRINCESS DRAGOMIROFF: *a Russian princess*

HILDEGARDE SCHMIDT: *her lady's maid*

GRETA OHLSSON: *a Swedish missionary*

COUNT AND COUNTESS ANDRENYI: *Hungarian royalty who are traveling first class*

Wrapping up some business that carried him to Syria, Poirot has booked his passage home on the famed Orient Express, a railway stretching from Stamboul (Istanbul) to Paris. On board, he notices that the train seems quite crowded for the winter season. What's more, the passengers come from all walks of life, and are all of varying nationalities. There's a Swedish missionary, a Hungarian count and countess, a Russian princess, an English colonel, and a German maid. There are also a few Americans on board, including the loud-mouthed American Mrs. Hubbard, as well as Hector MacQueen, who is the secretary to another American, the sour-faced businessman Mr. Ratchett.

As soon as Poirot notices Ratchett, he knows there is something he doesn't like about him. Ratchett tells Poirot that he is worried over recent threats to his life, and offers him the handsome sum of £20,000 to help investigate. Poirot refuses, saying, "If you will forgive me. . . I do not like your face."

That night, Poirot awakens a little before one in the morning. He hears a groan, and a bell summoning the conductor. He then notices a voice in French coming from Ratchett's sleeping compartment, saying, "It's nothing." Soon after, there's more commotion, this time from Mrs. Hubbard, who insists that a man was just in her room. The conductor, Pierre Michel, assures her that it must have been her imagination, but she remains adamant. Michel dismisses her, as he has more concerning matters to attend to: The train has just come to a complete standstill, blocked by a huge snowdrift on the tracks. The passengers are stranded somewhere in the Balkan countryside, and may be there for several days!

ALBERT FINNEY AND SUSPECTS IN
MURDER ON THE ORIENT EXPRESS, 1974

The next morning, Ratchett is found murdered in his bed, savagely stabbed twelve times. The door was locked and chained on the inside. There is a pocketwatch on the victim, stopped at 1:15 a.m., presumably shattered from one of the blows. What's most curious about the victim's stab wounds are that they are so varied: some have been dealt with great force, seemingly from a man of strength; others are shallow wounds, which could have been made by a woman. In addition, some have been administered by a right-handed person, while others may have come from the left-handed angle. Poirot wonders if there could be two murderers . . .

Poirot teams up with Monsieur Bouc, the director of the Wagon-Lit train company, to investigate the crime. Since they are stranded for the foreseeable future, they know the police may not arrive for quite some time. At the crime scene, they note that the window is open, but there are no footprints in the snow. The murderer couldn't have escaped. He or she must be on the train! There are only thirteen people on board, and Poirot must get to work questioning all of them.

But first, the most earth-shattering clue has been found in Ratchett's room: The remnants of a burned letter. It reveals Ratchett's true identity. He is a notorious

criminal named Cassetti! A couple
of years before, there had been
the famous case of the Armstrong
abduction in the headlines. Three-
year-old American heiress Daisy
Armstrong had been kidnapped.
Her family delivered a large ran-
som for her, but the child was
found brutally murdered. (Agatha
Christie based this plotline on the
Lindbergh baby kidnapping). Cassetti had been the child's murderer,
but he had been set free because

of a technicality. He emigrated
to Europe, while the Armstrong
family was left in shatters. Daisy's
mother, Sonia, had miscarried her
second child and died. Soon after
losing his wife and both children,
Colonel Armstrong died of grief.
Daisy's French nursemaid, Susanne,
had been so distraught over the
tragedy that she flung herself out
of a window. So Ratchett/Cassetti
had been responsible not only for
the unspeakable crime of killing an

innocent child, but also several sub-sequent deaths.

As Poirot questions the thir-teen passengers, he comes upon clues and evidence that seem to point in varying directions. It's all a muddle: Everyone is able to give an alibi for another person. There are clues that seem to have been planted, but all point to a different suspect. Many give testimony to having seen a mysterious woman wearing a scarlet kimono walk the hall about the time of the murder. Poirot then discovers the kimono hidden in his luggage, which is an indication that he is being challenged by a mastermind.

But in the end, even a mastermind, or even several masterminds, are no match for Poirot. He assembles everyone and offers two solutions. The first is that the culprit must have been a person that Ratchett had reported fearing: "A small dark man with a womanish

voice." That man must have stolen
a conductor's uniform, found a pass
key, and stabbed Ratchett in his
compartment. He went through
Mrs. Hubbard's door and escaped
off the train.

But then Poirot presents
another solution: There was not
a single murderer, but *all* the passengers on the train had killed
Ratchett. Everyone was hiding
their identity—and all had ties
to the Armstrong household.

The Countess was really Daisy's aunt. The Swede had been the Armstrong family's nurse. The Italian was the family chauffeur. Ratchett's valet had been Colonel Armstrong's war buddy. Hector MacQueen's father was the prosecuting attorney on the case. The train's conductor had been Susanne's father. And Mrs. Hubbard had been Daisy's grandmother, the renowned actress Linda Arden. She was playing the part of her life, as the obnoxious American who "saw" a getaway murderer.

The ruse almost worked. Twelve out of the thirteen passengers were Ratchett's executioners (twelve being a very fitting number, as they acted as Ratchett's jury). They drugged Ratchett, then each stole into his room and dealt a single blow with a dagger. No one would know which stab would be the fatal one—so the murder could not be pinned to a single person. The avenging crime was a group effort. It was also a group effort to confuse Poirot with the red herring of the "silk kimono" woman and the bevy of fake clues.

It was all so brilliant—but not brilliant enough to fool Poirot! After the renowned detective presents both theories, Bouc makes the decision to go with the first solution. Once the train gets moving and the Yugoslavian police arrive on the scene, Bouc will say that the murderer must have gotten away. Poirot respects their decision, and only says that he has "the honor to retire from the case."

The ABC Murders

(1936)

Hastings: *"What do you call the
unforgiveable error?"*

Poirot: *"Overlooking the obvious!"*

ALICE ASCHER: *a shopkeeper*

MARY DROWER: *her niece*

BETTY BARNARD: *a flirtatious waitress*

MEGAN BARNARD: *her sister*

DONALD FRASER: *Betty's long-suffering fiancé*

SIR CARMICHAEL CLARKE: *a wealthy man and third victim of ABC*

LADY CLARKE: *his wife, who is suffering from cancer*

FRANKLIN CLARKE: *Carmichael's boyishly handsome brother*

THORA GREY: *Carmichael's secretary —and perhaps something more?*

INSPECTOR CRONE: *co-investigator on the mysterious A.B.C. serial killer case*

Hastings writes an account of a strange case that took place in 1935. Returning to England from his ranch in Argentina, Hastings visits his dear *ami* Poirot, now living in posh digs in London. While there, a taunting letter arrives in the post:

"*You fancy yourself, don't you, at solving mysteries that are too difficult for our poor thick-headed British police?*" The letter then says to watch out for something to happen on the 21st at Andover. It is signed simply, "A.B.C." Both Hastings and Inspector Japp chalk up the note to a madman. Surely it's nothing to take seriously.

But on the 21st, Japp reports that there *has* been a murder. The victim is Alice Ascher, an old woman who ran a humble tobacco shop. Her body was founded huddled near the cash register, her head bashed in. No money was taken, so it wasn't a robbery. It's assumed that the culprit must be Mrs. Ascher's drunken husband—but there were no witnesses who can vouch for having seen him near the shop. Another curious thing about the case—an ABC Railway Guide was placed near Mrs. Ascher's body.

Poirot soon receives another letter from "A.B.C.," saying, "*The Andover business went with a swing, didn't it? The fun is only beginning. Let me draw your attention to Bexhill-on-Sea, the 25th.*"

Sure enough, a woman named Betty Barnard is found murdered in Bexhill on the appointed day. She was a pretty waitress who worked at a little tea shop called the Ginger Cat. Her body was found on the beach, where she was strangled with her own belt—once again, an ABC railway guide is left at the scene of the crime. Alice Ascher at Andover and Betty Barnard at Bexhill? The murderer is following the pattern of the alphabet!

Poirot is able to accompany the inspectors while they question the victim's family. They discover that Betty had a beau named Donald Fraser, an earnest, steady kind of fellow. But Betty also had a bit of a roving eye—she liked to have "a bit of fun" and go out with other suitors. Her own sister, Megan, admits that her sister was an "unmitigated little ass"—unquestionably a silly, thoughtless creature. Poirot notes that in both cases, there would have been a clear culprit if "ABC" hadn't bragged about the crimes. Mrs. Ascher's niece, Mary, had at first supposed that her "auntie" died at the hands of her husband. And in Betty's case, her jealous fiancé would have been strongly suspected.

Poirot then gets a third missive: "*Let us see if you can do any better this time,*" ABC writes teasingly, "*This time it's an easy one. Churston on the 30th.*" But this letter is different. Rather than receiving it a few days before the crime, Poirot receives it on the day of—too late for him to take any action. The delay was caused by the letter being wrongly addressed. ABC had erroneously written "Whitehorse Mansions" rather than "White-haven Mansions"—a seemingly natural blunder.

Hastings and Poirot rush to catch a train to Churston, where they are met by Inspectors Japp and Crone. Sir Carmichael Clarke has had his head bashed in, with an open ABC railway guide placed upon his body. Unlike the last two victims, Sir Carmichael Clarke had been a man of wealth and stature. At his impressive estate, Poirot and Inspector Crone interview the surviving family. There is his brother, Franklin, just returned from living in the Far East; Lady Clarke, who is suffering from incurable cancer; and Carmichael's attractive Swedish secretary, Thora Grey.

Hastings' narrative is then interrupted by third-person accounts of a traveling salesman named Alexander Bonaparte Cust. Though his mother had given him grand names (after Alexander the Great and Napoleon), his personality seems to be the direct opposite of his namesakes. Cust does not have the stuff of a brazen, charismatic leader, but rather he's weak-minded, jittery, and suffers from headaches. He seems to have recently traveled to Andover, Bexham, and now to Churston . . .

Back to Hasting's account of the investigation: The victims' families (Mary, Franklin, Megan, and Donald) all decide to meet to put their heads together. Maybe there was something each of them could remember? Some sort of clue that would unify the crimes and lead them to the culprit? They come up dry, but not without Poirot asking them a few pointed questions.

Poirot then pays a visit to Lady Clarke. Though heavily drugged on morphine, she is coherent enough to let Poirot know that there is something suspicious about Thora. Not only did Thora have designs on her husband, Lady Clarke reports, but on the day of the murder, she had seen Thora talking with a strange man. Yet Thora had firmly said that she had seen no one. Who is lying? When pressed further, Thora suddenly recalls talking with a rather nondescript gentleman, "He wasn't the sort of man you'd notice." He was a door-to-door salesman, selling women's stockings. Why, that's it! Before all the victims were killed, they had bought new stockings. That is the unifying clue!

Poirot gets a fourth let-ter—A.B.C. will strike at Doncaster on September 11th. A body is found, stabbed in a movie theater. But this time A.B.C. has made a mistake—the victim is identified as a George Easterfield. But a Mr. Downes had been sitting nearby— apparently A.B.C. has killed the wrong person.

The police get a tip from Alexander Cust's landlady— she has been reading about the crimes in the papers, and has realized her tenant has traveled to all of the towns where the murders were committed in the past few weeks. But the tip proves unnecessary, because Cust soon walks into the police station and turns himself in. He is an epileptic, and has suffered from seizures and blackouts ever since he returned from the war. He can't explain why he had a blood-stained coat the day of the "D" murder—but he knows he must have done it.

It seems an open-and-shut case—in addition to the confession, they found a stash of ABC railway guides in Cust's flat, and the letters

have been typed on his typewriter.
Yet holes appear in the seemingly
airtight case: One, Cust has a defi-
nite alibi for the night of Betty
Barnard's murder (playing domi-
noes in a hotel lobby). Two, Cust
denies having written to Poirot.
Three, Cust has no motive. Though
he is sure he must have done the
murders during his frequent blackouts, he has no idea *why*.

Poirot also has his doubts.
The "ABC" of the letters and

subsequent killings is cunning and ruthless, while Cust is stupid and wishy-washy. It's almost like the ABC murderer and Alexander Bonaparte Cust are two different men. . . Aha!

Poirot's "little grey cells" are able to piece everything together, and he gathers everyone to explain: ABC didn't fit the profile of a serial killer. Serial killers usually choose the same sort of victim. But ABC chose an old woman, a pretty girl, and an aging man. ABC also varied the method of death. But Betty Barnard's murder differed from the "A" and "C" murder, in that she was strangled, apparently by someone she had been canoodling with on the beach. She must have been seduced, and Alexander Cust certainly could not have tempted an attractive young woman. Since there was no way Cust could have done the "B" murder, then, Poirot logically follows, he didn't do *any* of them.

The real murderer was . . .
Franklin Clarke! He is attractive,
cunning, and resourceful. He
planned a series of murders to
distract investigators from the one
murder that would most certainly
benefit him: That of Carmichael Clarke. Franklin, a "boy at
heart," knew that his adventurous,
prodigal life has left him penniless—while his brother held
all the wealth. He was growing
increasingly resentful, and could

see the writing on the wall. Lady Clarke would soon succumb to her disease, and Carmichael would most certainly marry his pretty secretary, Thora, a woman young and vibrant enough to produce children. Those hypothetical children would inherit Carmichael's money—so Franklin wasn't going to take any chances. He needed to kill his brother to ensure his rightful inheritance. But how could he do it without being suspected?

While pondering a perfect crime, Franklin had randomly met the neurotic, highly suggestible Alexander Bonaparte Cust—and he knew he had found the perfect scapegoat. It all fell into place: He would create an "ABC" serial killer, and commit a series of crimes that would generate a lot of publicity. Carmichael would simply be considered another unfortunate victim of a mad killer, and Franklin would never fall under suspicion.

But this elaborate ruse took a lot of planning. Franklin offered Cust a job as a hosiery salesman, and gave him a traveling schedule. He was due to be in Andover on July 25th, and Bexhill a few days later, etc. He also told Cust that he would send the inventory to his flat. But the parcel contained not only women's stockings, but also a stash of ABC railway guides. Franklin also supplied him with a typewriter to help complete his tasks (the same typewriter used to write Poirot's letters).

Why was Poirot selected as the recipient of the letters, and not simply Scotland Yard? Because it's impossible to misaddress a letter to New Scotland Yard, but a simple mistake on the envelope to a private residence is not considered unusual. Franklin had to be sure that the "C" crime was carried off without a hitch—so he purposely flubbed Poirot's address on the third letter, so that the police would not be adequately warned.

Franklin didn't want to kill through the whole alphabet, so the "D" murder was deliberately meant to be a flub. He followed Cust into a darkened cinema. He killed someone randomly in the theater, and then collided with Cust so that there would be blood on his clothes. Cust, knowing he was in the right locations for all the murders, and being plagued with his affliction, would assume he was the murderer.

While recounting Franklin's method and motive, Poirot then tells a little fib. He informs Franklin that his fingerprint has been found on Cust's typewriter. Upon hearing that there is irrefutable proof of his culpability, Franklin tries to shoot himself in the head. But Poirot is one step ahead of him—he had already taken the bullets from Franklin's pistol.

No, Poirot muses, Franklin will not be able to escape punishment. Before Franklin is carted away, Poirot scolds him that his plan to frame Cust for the murders was not altogether *sporting*. Luckily for Alexander Bonaparte Cust, Poirot was on the case to hunt a wily villain!

Cards on the Table

(1936)

*"I collect only the best . . .
The criminals who lead an
agreeable life which no breath
of suspicion has ever touched"*

—Mr. Shaitana

❧ MAIN CHARACTERS ❧

MR. SHAITANA: *a collector of prized objects—including murderers*

DOCTOR ROBERTS: *a genial medical practitioner*

MRS. LORRIMER: *a smart woman who plays bridge with precision*

MAJOR DESPARD: *a rugged adventurer*

ANNE MEREDITH: *a shy young woman with a nervous nature*

RHODA DAWES: *her loose-lipped friend*

MRS. ARIADNE OLIVER: *the renowned authoress of mysteries*

COLONEL RACE: *a member of His Majesty's Secret Service*

SUPERINTENDENT BATTLE: *a Scotland Yard inspector*

Mr. Shaitana is considered a "Mephistophelean" man: Devilish in demeanor, with keen knowledge of the dark side. Most people admit to being a little afraid of him, but he gives the most smashing parties, so they can't resist his invitations. Shaitana is also quite a collector, his grand home full of beautiful pieces. He boasts to Poirot that he also likes to "collect" murderers: The best kind, he says, are the ones who have gotten away with it! He wants Poirot to marvel at his exhibits, so he arranges a dinner party where he'll invite four murderers. Shaitana explains to Poirot that these four people *think* they have been successful in committing their crimes without suspicion, so they won't know that they are "on display."

When the appointed evening arrives, Poirot sees that Mr. Shaitana has made the guest list even more intriguing by including three other experts in criminal behavior. In addition to Poirot, there is Mrs. Ariadne Oliver, the famed mystery novelist; Superintendent Battle, a Scotland Yard inspector; and Colonel Race, who works for the Secret Service.

Then there are the supposed murderers: Mrs. Lorrimer, a handsome, shrewd widow in her sixties; Major Despard, a virile man who has had many adventures in far-off lands; Doctor Roberts, who is described as cheerful, middle-aged and "well-scrubbed"; and Anne Meredith, a soft-spoken yet jittery young woman.

During dinner, Shaitana lets a few hints drop. He alludes to "secret woman poisoners," and remarks that "doctors also have opportunities to commit murders." After the meal, two different groups form to play bridge. As it happens, all the "murderers" are playing together in the drawing room, while the "crime experts" are placed in another room. Mr. Shaitana is the only one who sits the game out, settling himself in a big armchair by the drawing-room fireplace.

After everyone plays a few hands (or "rubbers," as they're called in bridge), Mr. Shaitana is discovered in the armchair, fatally stabbed with a thin, jeweled dagger from his own collection. Since no one else had entered or left the drawing room, the culprit must be one of the four "secret murderers"—acting while one of them sat out a dummy hand. Could one of them have felt threatened by Shaitana's hints at dinnertime? Who could be clever or brazen enough to commit murder in the middle of a bridge game?

To Poirot, the answer to that question can be approached from a few different angles. First, he examines the four suspects' personalities and the way they played bridge that evening. Doctor Roberts is rather a slapdash player. He is quick and takes big risks. In fact, he had called a grand slam during one of the rubbers. In stark contrast is Mrs. Lorrimer, who is sharp-as-a-tack, yet very methodical. She has a mathematical brain and remembers all of the plays in detail. Despard, meanwhile, doesn't remember anything in detail. And Miss Anne Meredith seems to play her cards rather timidly— just the way she plays her cards in life.

Second, Poirot teams with the other sleuths to delve into each of the suspects' pasts. Is there any evidence to support Shaitana's claims that they have committed murders? They soon dig up some dirt on Doctor Roberts. He apparently had an inappropriate relationship with one of his patients, a Mrs. Craddock. Her jealous husband had threatened to ruin Roberts' career. After the two men quarreled, Mr. Craddock died after using an infected shaving brush. Soon after, his wife died of fever in Egypt—even though Doctor Roberts gave her a typhoid inoculation before she left on the trip. Mighty fishy indeed!

Alas, there doesn't seem to be anything suspicious about Mrs. Lorrimer. Apart from the fact that her husband died more than twenty years before, she seems to have led an exemplary life.

It's clear that Anne Meredith is hiding something, and clever Mrs.

Oliver finds out what. She craftily questions Anne's very talkative friend, Rhoda Dawes. It doesn't take much to get Rhoda to blab the whole story: Anne is an army officer's daughter, very respectable but penniless. She supports herself by being a proper companion to elderly ladies. A few years before, one of her former employers met an untimely demise—some leftover hat paint had been put into a cough syrup bottle. The maid must have carelessly moved around the bottles and the old woman had inadvertently ingested the poison. It was all very unfortunate. Anne had been living at the house at the time, but there had never been even a whisper of suspicion about her. Though, Rhoda admits, it *is* a little strange that Anne failed to mention the incident when she was being questioned after Shaitana's death. Why is she being so cagey?

The sleuths then dig up something from Major Despard's past: He had been accompanying a botanist named Professor Luxmore and his wife in South America. The professor had died suddenly, supposedly of fever. Poirot questions Mrs. Luxmore, now living in London. It doesn't take much prodding for her to spill the beans. She claims that Major Despard had fallen passionately in love with her, and shot her husband dead when they were in the remote Amazon jungle.

After Poirot recounts Mrs. Luxmore's story to Major Despard, Despard has nothing but disdain for "that damned fool of a woman." He refutes her story, saying that she had been under a delusion that he had a mad passion for her. Her husband, meanwhile, had been in a fever delirium and had waded into the Amazon. In an effort to stop him from drowning himself, Major Despard had taken his rifle and aimed at Luxmore's leg, intending just to lame him. But, in a dramatic flourish, Mrs. Luxmore had grabbed Despard's arm right at the critical moment, causing him to accidentally make a fatal shot. Poirot is inclined to believe his side of the story— Major Despard is an accidental murderer. He isn't the kind to premeditate anything, and Poirot knows he didn't stab Shaitana.

Poirot lays a crafty trap for Anne, and confirms that she is a petty thief (she has nicked a couple of pairs of expensive hosiery). This solidifies his keen analysis of her personality, and of her crime: Anne is sneaky and underhanded, as well as timid and indirect. In switching around bottles, she completed the murder of her employer. But could meek Anne do anything so bold as to stab a man with three potential eyewitnesses in the room? It doesn't seem to fit her nature.

Mrs. Lorrimer asks Poirot to visit her, and states that she was the one who murdered Mr. Shaitana! He knew that she had killed her husband many years ago, and she felt she had to get rid of him. Poirot doesn't believe this confession. After all, he relies on his "little grey cells" and of the psychological profiles he has compiled on each of the suspects. Mrs. Lorrimer is methodical, and would be more likely to commit a crime that required precise planning. But impetuously stabbing a man while others were in the room? Not a chance. Mrs. Lorrimer relents—she is a dying woman, and has no future before her. She wants to take the blame for sweet, young Anne. Mrs. Lorrimer explains that she had seen Anne approach Shaitana's armchair while she played "dummy" during one of the rubbers, and the two women had made eye contact. Poirot wants justice served if indeed Anne is guilty, but Mrs. Lorrimer tells Poirot that she will deny ever having this conversation with him.

The next morning, Mrs. Lorrimer is found dead from an apparent suicide. Before taking a lethal dose of veronal, she had written notes to each of the remaining suspects, confessing to Shaitana's murder. Doctor Roberts was the first to receive the confession in the morning post, and he had immediately rushed to her bedside to see if he could save her, but it was too late. The police discover that Anne had visited Mrs. Lorrimer the night before. She must have administered the veranol. Seems that Anne is a very dangerous woman, and she must be stopped!

Poirot and Battle, along with Major Despard, race to find Anne. They see her punting on the river with Rhoda. Then they clearly witness her push Rhoda overboard. Poirot knows that Anne must be desperate to silence her blabbermouth friend who knows of her suspicious past. Anne is pulled overboard as well, and struggles in the reeds. Major Despard valiantly saves Rhoda, but Anne drowns. Seems it's an open-and-shut case—it must have been Anne who killed Shaitana and Mrs. Lorrimer. But as always, Poirot is one step ahead . . .

The culprit was not Anne, but rather Doctor Roberts. Poirot had hired an undercover "window cleaner," who witnessed the doctor shooting something into Mrs. Lorrimer's arm on the morning she died. The suicide notes were forgeries.

Poirot arrived at the solution based on a few factors. Doctor Roberts' personality profile, the way he carried out the Craddocks' murders, and the way he played bridge on that fateful night. Doctor Roberts' basic M.O. is to make bold, audacious moves. He takes a big gamble but plays his cards well. For example, during the bridge game Doctor Roberts had called a grand slam, which suddenly made the rubber have very high stakes. He sat out "dummy" for that round, while all the other players were concentrating on their cards. This provided him with the needed distraction to kill Shaitana. It was a daring move and one done in public, which was very similar to the way Doctor Roberts had boldly carried out his other murders. He had gone into Mr. Craddock's bathroom and laced his shaving brush with anthrax. Soon after, he had given Mrs. Craddock her "inoculation" in front of others, and it would make her very ill a few days later.

But why was Mrs. Lorrimer so convinced that she saw Anne murder Shaitana? Mrs. Lorrimer had only seen Anne go to where Shaitana sat near the fireplace. Anne was the first to discover that Shaitana was dead, but she remained silent out of fear. She was nervous that she was now a suspect, and that the police would start digging into her past.

Meanwhile, Doctor Roberts had no idea that Mrs. Lorrimer thought Anne was the murderer. He only knew that the aging woman was very ill and not long for the world, so she would be the perfect scapegoat. He forged the suicide notes, and sent one to his own address. Receiving Mrs. Lorrimer's full "confession" in the morning post gave him the perfect excuse to barge into her bedroom in an attempt to "revive" her. He told the maid to fetch the police, which gave him ample time to give her a deadly injection.

His bold moves almost paid off—but his gambler's luck was no match for Poirot. As Poirot says on the last page, "He has thrown his cards upon the table. *C'est fini*."

Death on the Nile

(1937)

*"I suppose you believe it
would be very wrong to kill a
person who has injured you—
even if they've taken away everything
you had in the world?"*

—Jackie De Bellefort

❧ MAIN CHARACTERS ❧

LINNET RIDGEWAY: *a rich and beautiful heiress—she takes what she wants, when she wants it*

JACQUELINE "JACKIE" DE BELLEFORT: *her best friend*

SIMON DOYLE: *the man that comes between them*

MRS. SALOME OTTERBOURNE: *a flamboyant authoress of scandalous novels*

ROSALIE OTTERBOURNE: *her long-suffering, sulky daughter*

TIM ALLERTON: *an affable young man who seems suspicious about having Poirot around*

MISS MARIE VAN SCHUYLER: *an altogether unpleasant woman*

NURSE BOWERS: *the ever patient (and discreet) attendant to Miss Van Schuyler*

CORNELIA ROBSON: *the cousin and companion to Miss Van Schuyler*

ANDREW PENNINGTON: *Linnet's American estate agent*

COLONEL RACE: *after helping Poirot in the* Cards on the Table *mystery, he makes another appearance— in Egypt*

LOUISE: *Linnet's French maid— who sees a little too much for her own good*

DR. BESSNER: *a German physician who is enjoying a holiday*

MR. RICHETTI: *an Italian archeologist (or is he?)*

JIM FANTHORP: *a man who seems to be lurking around for some purpose*

Twenty-year-old heiress Linnet Ridgeway has it all: money, power, and looks. And what she doesn't have, she simply takes. In fact, she has just taken her best friend's fiancé. When Jacqueline de Bellefort told her oldest pal that she had fallen desperately in love with handsome Simon Doyle, she asked if Linnet could possibly give him a job. Jackie confided to Linnet that she'd simply die if she couldn't marry him—but the only glitch in the union was that he didn't have a penny to his name. As soon as Linnet took a look at Simon, she gave him a job alright . . . she made Simon her husband!

Now, a few months later, Linnet and Simon are on their honeymoon in Egypt, taking a cruise up the Nile. Several other people are on the excursion as well. Most are on a holiday, but others have an ulterior motive for being there. There is Hercule Poirot, of course, as well

Colonel Race, who is investigating a possible terrorist onboard. There's the novelist Salome Otterbourne, infamous for her steamy novels, and her daughter Rosalie; American heiress Marie Van Schuyler, traveling with her nurse, Miss Bowers, and her companion, Cornelia Robson; the breezy young man Tim Allerton with his mother; Andrew Pennington, Linnet's American estate agent who "just happens" to show up on Linnet's honeymoon; the mysterious

Jim Fanthorp; Italian archeologist Mr. Richetti; and Dr. Bessner, a German physician. The last traveler is none other than . . . Jackie!

Since being jilted by her lover and betrayed by her best friend, she has decided the best course of revenge is to follow them on their honeymoon. She seems rather pleased that she has rattled Linnet and upset Simon—but wise Poirot tells her not to open her heart to evil. Jackie admits that she would like to "put my dear little pistol close against [Linnet's] head" . . . and pull the trigger.

One day, the boat docks and the travelers stroll among the Egyptian ruins. Everyone is in awe of the temples. Along the trail, a boulder comes loose and narrowly misses Linnet. Was it an accident of nature, or something deliberate? But Jackie was nowhere near the boulder when it happened. Could Linnet have *other* enemies?

The next evening Poirot retires early, feeling very sleepy. But others stay up: Jacqueline orders a double gin in the ship's saloon, then knocks back a few more. At first she engages in conversation with the meek and mild Cornelia, but then loudly taunts Simon, "Do you think you can treat me as you've done and get away with it?" Fanthorp, the only other person witnessing this scene, tries to excuse himself.

Suddenly, a drunken Jackie takes out a pistol from her purse and shoots Simon, hitting him in the leg. She is immediately aghast at what's she's done. Simon seems more worried for *her* than about his injury. He coolly instructs Cornelia to fetch Nurse Bowers to attend to Jackie, then he tells Fanthorp to get Dr. Bessner to have a look at his wound. He is left alone for a few minutes in the saloon, writhing in pain before the doctor comes. It's now past midnight, and Simon is adamant that his wife not know about this terrible scene just yet.

In fact, she never will know because the next morning, Linnet is found in her bed, shot through the head! There are burn marks on her skin, indicating that someone put a pistol right to her temple while she was sleeping, and pulled the trigger. Time of death is between midnight and 2 a.m. Someone had written the letter "J" in blood on the wall—which casts suspicion on Jackie. But she couldn't have been the culprit since Nurse Bowers gave her a tranquilizer soon after her attack on Simon.

As Poirot and Colonel Race start their queries, more curious things arise: Miss Van Schuyler's missing velvet stole is retrieved from the river, along with Jackie's pistol. The stole has a bullet hole through it, so it must have been used as a silencer. The Allertons both say that they heard running footsteps and a splash in the middle of the night. Rosalie was spotted throwing something overboard— but she denies it vehemently. Could she have been the one to throw the incriminating weapon over- board? She certainly seems like an unhappy girl with a burden on her shoulders. What could it be?

Linnet's maid, Louise, also seems to know something, but upon being questioned she clams up. Simon reassures her, "my good girl. You'll be quite all right. . . . Nobody's accusing you of anything."

Another issue that gums up the investigation: Linnet's pearls, appraised at about £50,000, have gone missing. They soon turn up— Nurse Bowers explains that Miss Van Schuyler is a kleptomaniac, and hopes that Poirot and Race will be discreet and not expose the family to any scandal. But when Poirot examines the pearls supposedly belonging to Linnet, he knows they are fakes—someone must have switched out the real pearls at some point during the cruise. Could Linnet have discovered the ruse? Were the pearls a possible motive for murder?

Dr. Beemer says that Simon's injury isn't that serious, but they should get him to a hospital soon for treatment. There is a chance he could die of infection, or be permanently disabled. Jackie is racked with guilt, but Simon soon sends for her and soothes her worries. They are left alone for a little while—and Poirot muses that when the Sun (Linnet) fades, the Moon (Jackie) is all the more visible. Perhaps the old lovers might be reconciled eventually?

Poirot examines everyone's cabins. He finds an empty bottle of red nail polish in Linnet's room. He spots a rosary in Tim Allerton's room. Then he goes to search

DAVID NIVEN AS COLONEL RACE,
USTINOV AS POIROT, ANGELA LANSBURY
AS MRS. SALOME OTTERBOURNE, OLIVIA
HUSSEY AS ROSALIE OTTERBOURNE

Louise's room—where he finds her body stashed under the bed! She has been stabbed with one of Dr. Bessner's surgical instruments. She still has money clutched in her hand—she must have been blackmailing the murderer!

Soon after, Mrs. Otterbourne makes a dramatic scene. She announces to everyone that she knows who killed Louise and Linnet. She plays her big scene for all it's worth, telling her story slowly, saying she saw who went into the maid's cabin. Just as her lips form to reveal the name—a shot comes out of nowhere and shoots her dead! Both Poirot and Colonel Race scurry to catch the culprit, all to no avail.

It doesn't take long for Poirot to solve the smaller mysteries and expose the lesser scoundrels aboard the ship. Pennington was indeed trying to swindle Linnet of some of her assets, and tried to get her to sign some papers. Jim Fanthorp was sent as a watchdog from her English solicitors, to make sure that Pennington didn't succeed in cheating Linnet out of her money. Pennington was the one who "accidentally" dislodged the boulder. He desperately thought that if business-minded Linnet were out of the way, then it would be more likely for her hapless husband to give Pennington control of her estate.

Tim Allerton is exposed as a petty jewel thief. He was in on a heist to rob rich folks of their precious jewelry by switching them out with good replicas. Linnet's real pearls are hidden in his hollow rosary!

Poirot lets Tim go free. At heart, Tim is really a good guy who is clearly in love with Rosalie. Poor Rosalie, who had to hide her mother's alcoholism, and even dumped her mother's stash of liquor overboard. Tim promises to give up his thieving ways in return for Rosalie's heart. A couple of

other loose plot strands are sewn
up: Richietti is revealed to be part
of the terrorist plot that Race was
investigating. Cornelia, whose
father lost a fortune on account of
Linnet's father, finds happiness with
Dr. Beamer.

But who murdered Lin-
net, then later Louise and Mrs.
Otterbourne? Poirot now sees it
clearly—and knows that Linnet's
murder was carefully planned
and orchestrated . . . not just by

one murderer, but by two. The murderers were, in fact, Simon and Jackie! They had carried out a brilliant plan—one that gave them airtight alibis. After all, when Linnet was killed, Simon was suffering with a gashing wound to his leg, while Jackie had been tranquilized. Or were they? Here's how it really went:

Simon and Jackie were both very much in love. But Simon had always wanted to be rich. When he first met Linnet, he had mused to Jackie that it would be ideal if he could just marry Linnet and have her "die within a year, and then leave me all the boodle." Simon certainly didn't have the brains to pull off an elaborate murder, but Jackie did. She let Linnet "steal" Simon away from her (Linnet was particularly callous and entitled about this). Then they orchestrated this plan whereby Jackie would act like the mad jilted lover. The night of the murder, they drugged Poirot's wine so that he would be asleep and not interfere with their scheme. They staged the quarrel in the saloon, and Jackie pretended to shoot Simon in the leg. Simon used red nail polish to feign a wound. While Jackie was escorted out of the room and the doctor was summoned, Simon had the critical few minutes needed to commit the crime. Simon grabbed Jackie's pistol, ran to his wife's room, and killed her (and he couldn't help the added flourish of the blood-written "J"). He had put the gun right against Linnet's skin, which accounted for the burns on her temple. So a silencer wasn't used for the bullet that killed Linnet. But the velvet stole *was* used as a silencer for the next shot—the one that Simon self-afflicted to his leg. He then flung the stole and pistol overboard (thus accounting for the footsteps and splash sounds heard by the other passengers).

Later, when the maid gave her testimony, Simon knew that she was hinting that she had seen him go into his wife's cabin at the time of the murder. So he summoned Jackie to his bedside, and told her that she had to get rid of the maid—and quickly. But Jackie wasn't counting on Mrs. Otterbourne seeing her go into Louise's cabin. Jackie had to kill twice to cover her tracks. As she tells Poirot, she opened her heart to evil, and

she found it surprisingly easy
to murder.

In the end, Jackie takes fate into
her hands: She shoots Simon out of
love, because she knows he couldn't
stand to go to the gallows. Then she
turns the gun upon herself. Justice
and mercy are both served.

Evil Under the Sun

(1941)

"I have seen another evil under the sun, and it weighs heavily on mankind."

—Ecclesiastes 6: 1-5

❧ MAIN CHARACTERS ❧

ARLENA STUART MARSHALL: *a glamorous actress and purported seductress*

KENNETH MARSHALL: *her stiff-upper-lip husband*

LINDA MARSHALL: *Arlena's step-daughter*

PATRICK REDFERN: *a handsome young man who finds himself besotted by the siren Arlena*

CHRISTINE REDFERN: *his pale wife, not suited to a holiday in the sun*

HORACE BLATT: *another guest at the hotel—a supposed "self-made" man*

ROSAMUND DARNLEY: *Kenneth's old childhood friend*

EMILY BREWSTER: *a spinster*

ALICE CORRIGAN: *the victim of an unsolved crime*

Poirot has come to spend a holiday at the Jolly Roger resort, a beautiful place situated on an island off the Devon coast. The hotel sits upon a cliff, while the shoreline is dotted with hidden coves, a perfect place for sunbathing enthusiasts. It's a pity for Christine Redfern, a quiet, delicate young woman who blisters in the sun, and must wear flowing caftans and floppy hats for protection. Her husband is quite the Adonis: He's lean, bronzed, and has an infatuation with another guest at the hotel, the actress Arlena Stuart Marshall. Mrs. Marshall has a reputation for being a vixen. With a gorgeous figure and beautiful tan, it's no wonder she can beguile men. She's come to the Jolly Roger with her husband, Kenneth Marshall, and her sixteen-year-old step-daughter, Linda. Other guests at the resort include Emily Brewster, a gruff, no-nonsense woman; Horace Blatt, a red-faced man with a penchant for sailing; and Rosamund Darnley, a friendly, successful, and sophisticated lady, as well as being Kenneth's old childhood friend.

It's quite clear to everyone at the Jolly Roger that Patrick Redfern and Arlena Marshall have met before, and have arranged to be at the resort for a lover's rendezvous. They hardly conceal their lust for one another, much to the chagrin of both of their spouses. In fact, Poirot overhears Christine and

Patrick having a spat about the issue. The collective wisdom is that Patrick has foolishly fallen for a "Jezebel," while Christine is the poor wife who must endure her husband's brazen infidelity.

On a gloriously clear and sunny day, Linda rises to go for an early morning swim. Upon her return, she's asked by Christine if she wants to accompany her to Gull Cove, which is a nice little spot for sketching and more swimming. They set off at about 10:30 a.m. Poirot is also up early, and sees Arlena setting off to paddle around the island. Arlena begs him not to tell anyone that he saw her—she says she just wants to be alone. But judging from the anticipatory look on her face, Poirot assumes she is going to meet her lover. That assumption proves to be wrong because Patrick soon appears, asking if anyone has seen Arlena. He seems forlorn that his lover has deserted him.

Emily Brewster returns from her morning dip in the ocean, and reports that she almost got conked on the head with a bottle that flew from one of the hotel windows. Who would do such a thing? Patrick then asks Emily to go for a ride with him on a rowboat. As they approach the secluded Pixy's Cove, they see Arlena Marshall. She's lying on the beach, her bronzed limbs outstretched, with a jade Chinese hat over her face. Patrick senses something is wrong, and rushes to her. He lifts up the hat and sees that she has been strangled. Patrick instructs Emily to go for help immediately—he'll stay with the body. After all, the murderer may still be lurking! Emily says she'll fetch help by going by rowboat. Though there is a faster way to the hotel—a steep steel ladder going up the cliff—it's not for the faint of heart. One would have to be very athletic and brave to attempt the treacherous climb.

Soon the Inspector is called in and everyone must account for their whereabouts between 10:15, about the time Arlena set off on her float, and 11:45, when her body was discovered. Linda and Christine can certainly account for one another. In fact, Christine distinctly asked Linda for the time right before she left Gull Cove. She had to dash at 11:45 in order to make a scheduled tennis date with Kenneth and Rosamund.

Kenneth says that he was typing business letters in his room from 10:40 until right before his tennis game at noon. But no one can back up his alibi, until Rosamund later recalls that she had popped her head in and saw him busily immersed in his tasks. It's clear that Rosamund carries a torch for her old school chum. Is she protecting him?

The police assume that the murderer must be a man. It took a man's strength to produce the horrific bruises around Arlena's neck. On the other "hand," so to speak, Linda Marshall is a big-boned teenager. There were queer things discovered in Linda's grate in her room—a pin, candle wax, and some burnt animal matter of some kind. Linda couldn't have gone on an early morning swim as she reported, because the maid noticed her bathing costume was dry at 9 a.m. Christine also says that Linda was carrying a parcel of candles that morning, and had an overall guilty demeanor. All of these facts don't add up—but Linda does have an air-tight alibi—swimming in Gull Cove, while Christine looked on. Still, the question remains: Could Linda have hated her stepmother so much that she would resort to murder?

There are other curious matters that arise. Christine says she overheard a conversation with Arlena and an unidentified man—there was a mention of blackmail. Indeed, Arlena had inherited £50,000 from a former paramour, and her lawyers confirm that her account is down to just £15,000. Who was bilking her out of a fortune? Was Arlena going to meet her blackmailer that fateful morning? Also, why would she be sunbathing at Pixy's Cove in the morning? After all, the cove only gets afternoon sun. When the police and Poirot go to explore the area, they discover a cave, with Arlena's distinctive perfume still wafting in the staid air. They also find a hidden box stashed with traces of heroin! Did Arlena happen upon a drug-smuggling scheme, thus needing to be silenced?

One more piece of strange testimony: The hotel maid insists she heard someone running a bath right before noon. An odd time to be bathing. Plus, none of the hotel guests said they'd taken a bath at that hour. Why?

Poirot examines other recent cases of strangulation in the district, and reads about an unsolved crime concerning a woman named Alice Corrigan. Her body was discovered by a female hiker, and the husband had a cast-iron alibi. Are the two cases somehow related?

Poirot asks everyone to a picnic, where he observes many guests happily skipping over the rocks, including the dainty Christine Redfern. Upon their return, they discover that Linda has taken an overdose of sleeping pills, and has left a note confessing to the murder. But Hercule Poirot is not fooled!

The crime and the way it was executed is now crystal-clear in his mind. Arlena did not really prey upon men. Rather, she was their prey. She was susceptible to seducers who took her money, and the smoothest of them all was Patrick Redfern. Arlena didn't have a black-mailer per se, but she had a lover who convinced her to loan him money to place in "investments" for her. Patrick had drained her of thousands of pounds and he knew it was only a matter of time before Kenneth found out. Patrick and his accomplice, Christine, worked out a perfect plan to do away with Arlena.

Upon arrival at the Jolly Roger, she and Patrick had staged

some marital rows to make it seem like Christine was a withering, wronged wife. Christine was not the delicate flower she seemed to be, but an athletic woman with the stamina to climb steep ladders and run quickly.

On the morning of the murder, Patrick and Arlena arranged to meet at Pixy's Cove. She had been a bit nervous that their rendezvous would be discovered by her husband, but Patrick gave her strict orders to hide in the cave if she heard anyone coming. Meanwhile, Christine stole into Linda's room early in the morning and adjusted her wristwatch forward twenty minutes. Soon after she ran into Linda and made their 10:30 date for Gull Cove, then went to her room to apply a bottle of fake suntan. She couldn't risk the bottle being traced to her, so she chucked it out the window (narrowly missing Emily's head!). She then dressed in long, flowing robes to hide her tan (having established that she must protect herself from the sun). Later, when she left Gull Cove, she pointedly asked Linda the time—11:45. As soon as Linda's head was turned, she set the watch to the correct time. Since it was really 11:25, she had time to run, strip off her caftan, then scramble down the ladder to Pixy's Cove. She prostrated herself on the sand and placed the hat atop her head to hide her face.

When Patrick and Emily approached in the rowboat, it was show time! It was a great performance: With a suntan, Christine's lithe limbs looked very much like Arlena's. Patrick "discovered" the body, pretended to be horrified, and sent Emily off for help. Once Emily was safely out of sight, Christine scrambled up the ladder and went to the hotel to wash off her fake suntan—in time to make her noontime tennis match. Meanwhile,

Arlena had obediently hidden in the cave when she saw Christine come down the ladder. Patrick met her in the hideaway, embraced her, strangled her, then laid her in the same sunbathing spot. It was the perfect crime!

How convenient that Linda was already feeling guilty for attempting a spell to harm her step-mother. She had consulted a book on witchcraft and performed a rit-ual that involved candles, a piece of

Arlena's hair, and a pin. Linda was the perfect scapegoat to take the fall for the crime. Christine even used the power of suggestion and told her where she kept her sleeping pills. An evil woman, indeed!

The wicked duo of Patrick and Christine Redfern had struck before. Poor Alice Corrigan had married "Edward" and taken out a handsome life insurance policy on herself. Patrick had strangled Alice after a female hiker (Christine) had supposedly discovered her body. It was another case of misdirecting the authorities on the time of death, and constructing unassailable alibis. They were brilliant, but not brilliant enough to outsmart Hercule Poirot.

Luckily, Linda survives her suicide attempt, and Kenneth realizes that he loves his old friend Rosamund (after all, she loves him enough to lie to the police to give him an alibi). Linda will have a stepmother she likes for a change! Horace Blatt is revealed to be part of a drug-smuggling ring, as all of his solitary sailing jaunts were a bit suspicious. As for Poirot, it seems he'll need a holiday from his holiday—there's no escape from evil, even in idyllic places.

Curtain: Poirot's Last Case

(1975)

*"Everyone is a potential murderer—
in everyone there arises from time to
time the wish to kill—
though not the will to kill."*

— Poirot

❖ MAIN CHARACTERS ❖

JUDITH HASTINGS: *Captain Hasting's daughter, a very serious and smart young woman*

DR. FRANKLIN: *a brilliant but frustrated scientist*

BARBARA FRANKLIN: *his invalid wife*

NURSE CRAVEN: *Barbara's caretaker*

SIR WILLIAM BOYD CARRINGTON: *Barbara's former suitor, now a very attractive widower*

MAJOR ALLERTON: *a handsome man with a bad reputation*

COLONEL AND DAISY LUTTRELL: *the current owners of Styles Manor*

STEPHEN NORTON: *an unassuming man, fond of bird-watching*

ELIZABETH COLE: *a pleasant spinster*

Poirot writes to longtime friend Arthur Hastings, calling for a reunion at Styles, the place where they solved their first mystery more than thirty years before. Hastings has been living in Argentina for many years, and is recently widowed. On this trip back to England, he is heartened that he will be reunited not only with his old friend Poirot, but also with his twenty-one-year-old daughter, Judith, who will be there with her employer, Dr. Franklin, and his wife, Barbara.

When Hastings arrives at Styles, he finds it much changed. Like many stately old homes in England, it has been converted to a guest house. The plumbing may be more modern, but Hastings can't help but feel sad that the home's former glory is gone.

Styles isn't the only thing that has changed for the worse—Poirot has aged considerably since Hastings last saw him. He's sick, feeble, and confined to a wheelchair. Still, his old "grey cells" are in good working order, and he informs Hastings he had an ulterior motive for calling him to Styles. He wants his help in catching a culprit! He presents Hastings with the case studies of five seemingly unrelated murders. Each one seems like an open-and-shut case, and each involves a person who goes "over the edge" and kills—for example, one is a case of a daughter killing a cruel father, another of a cuckolded husband killing his adulterous wife, another of a caretaker doing away with her over-demanding charge, etc. But in all five cases, there is a single person (referred to as "X") who was involved in the periphery. To be in the vicinity of five unrelated murders seems too much of a coincidence, is it not? What's more, he tells Hastings, "X" is currently under Styles' roof, and he expects there will be another murder soon.

Hastings is frustrated with his old friend. Why doesn't he just tell him who the murderer is? Poirot refuses, saying that to reveal X's identity would place Hastings in danger. After all, Hastings has always been a bit of an open book, incapable of a poker face—X would immediately know he/she is under suspicion. Poirot simply says he needs Hastings to be his "eyes and ears" on the case. Since Poirot is now a convalescent, he needs Hastings now more than ever.

Hastings gets familiar with the other guests at Styles. First, there are the proprietors of the guest house, Colonel Luttrell and his wife, Daisy. It is common knowledge that they are struggling for money, their budgets stretched to keep Styles afloat. It's a far cry from the Colonel's glory days, when he was a brave and strapping soldier in India. Now he's a near-penniless, henpecked husband. There's Miss Elizabeth Cole, a pleasant but melancholy woman in her mid-thirties; Sir William Boyd Carrington, an all-around "sporting chap" according to Hastings; Stephen Norton, a mild-mannered birdwatcher; and Major Allerton, a handsome man who seems a little too smooth with the ladies. Hastings takes an immediate dislike to Allerton.

Hastings is very happy to see his beloved daughter again, but admits he's a little afraid of her. She is so intense and serious about the world! Having completed a university education, she is now a laboratory assistant to Franklin. Both she and Franklin are totally committed to his research. According to Judith, Franklin's brilliant career has been stymied because of his wife, Barbara. A weak, sickly, flighty creature, Barbara is totally dependent on Franklin—and what's more, she doesn't take any interest in his work. Judith can hardly contain her disdain for Barbara, thinking her a very useless human being.

Barbara's caretaker, Nurse Craven, suggests that her patient isn't as sick as she seems. She certainly enjoys the attention of being a "damsel in distress." Barbara is especially keen to see her old childhood friend Boyd Carrington, who is now a handsome and rich widower. Hastings learns that Boyd Carrington had once been in love with Barbara, and now finds it disgraceful that she's married to someone who doesn't appreciate her.

The guests at Styles pass the evening with a game of bridge. Daisy Luttrell gives her husband a tongue-lashing over his poor playing skills. Norton whispers to Hastings, "It gets my back up to see that poor old boy bullied like that . . . Poor chap." Colonel Luttrell overhears the remark, and is further humiliated by knowing he's being pitied by his male peers.

The next day, the men are again spending time together, when Norton says that he's thirsty. Luttrell, ever the gracious host, goes to get some whiskey. But Daisy chides him for his extravagant ways, giving away expensive liquor to the guests. She scolds him and puts the whiskey back in the cabinet. Everyone is embarrassed for the Colonel.

Daisy walks out to the fields, while the men practice shooting wood pigeons. Luttrell takes his rifle, aims, and accidentally shoots his wife! Despite it being a horrific and bloody accident, she will pull through, as the wound hit her shoulder, not her heart. Luttrell seems absolutely shattered that he nearly killed his wife—after the accident, they both show affection for one another. Yet . . . everyone can't help but wonder, was it really an accident? Could Colonel Luttrell have meant to kill her? Hastings recalls the other cases involving X. If the Colonel had killed his wife, his case would be very similar to the others. When Hastings reports the unfortunate wounding of Daisy Luttrell, Poirot is sure that X has struck again!

Soon after, there is an intense conversation over the hypothetical subject of euthanasia. When is it justified? Judith rather callously says that, "unfit lives, useless lives, they should be got out of the way." In her opinion, able-bodied, useful persons should take the responsibility to make that decision, if needed. In fact, it's their duty. Norton praises her youthful spirit, but says, "you wouldn't have the courage when it came to it." Judith looks defiant.

Meanwhile, there is another potential scandal brewing. It's common knowledge that Allerton is a scoundrel. He has recently "ruined" a girl who later committed suicide. Norton tells Hastings that he should warn Judith about him, as the two seem to be enjoying a little flirtation. Judith is incensed when her father meddles in her love life—after all, she is a grown woman capable of handling her own affairs!

Hastings seethes with loathing for Allerton. He is quite convinced that he must be X! What's

more, Norton has seen something
through his binoculars while
bird-watching—but he refused to
let Hastings see. Could he have
spotted an assignation between
Judith and Allerton?

Hastings' dark tendencies
come to the surface—the scoundrel must be stopped! He must
protect his daughter! He steals
some sleeping pills from Allerton's
medicine chest, then dissolves them
in a cocktail. He will simply wait

for Allerton to come back for the evening . . . and he will suggest a nightcap . . . it will be so easy to do away with the cad. But first, Hastings goes in to check on Poirot, who offers him some cocoa. He politely accepts the rich concoction, and soon he falls asleep . . .

In the clear light of day, Hastings realizes how foolish and irrational he has been, nearly driven to murder! He can't believe that he, normally so easygoing and accommodating, almost killed a man. Hastings is relieved that he came to his senses. Even better, it looks like Judith and Allerton are not stealing away together, after all.

Meanwhile, Barbara is feeling a bit better. She had been rather put out that there was another sick person (Daisy) who was getting all the attention. She wants to host a little gathering, and serves everyone coffee in her boudoir. She praises her brilliant husband, saying he would risk anything in the name of science. He is so devoted to his work! Boyd Carrington sweeps her up playfully and takes her to the veranda to watch fireworks. Hastings gets a little misty—he misses his wife so much. To distract himself from his woes, he spins around the revolving bookcase table and browses for an interesting book. Everyone comes back and drinks their coffee.

Barbara dies that night. She has taken poison. It is ruled that it must have been suicide, largely on account of Poirot's testimony at the inquest. He had seen the deceased with a bottle of medication, and he substantiates that she was a depressed individual who had threatened suicide recently. Hastings sees that this testimony has drained Poirot—he looks even more sickly than before. His valet confirms that Poirot has had a series of little heart attacks and keeps little tablets by his bed to help him through these difficult bouts. It's only a matter of days or weeks—the end is near.

Though Barbara's death is ruled a suicide, things are looking a little fishy. Franklin doesn't seem sad at all over his wife's death. In fact, he openly admits he feels quite free. Judith seems devoted to Franklin's work . . . could she also be devoted to Franklin? Her callous judgment of useless lives is recalled . . . was this a case of justified euthanasia? Doing away with one useless life so that Franklin can fulfill his potential?

Norton confides to Hastings that he has seen something he shouldn't have seen, and he's not sure if he should tell. Hastings suggests he consult Poirot on the matter. It's arranged that Norton will come up to visit Poirot's room that evening, and that they'll have a private conversation. When Hastings retires to bed, he spots Norton in his rather ostentatious bathrobe, coming from the bathroom.

The next morning, Norton is found dead. He shot himself square in the middle of the forehead. The wound is perfectly symmetrical, and it's a little unusual to have this precise wound in cases of suicide. But then, what else could it be? Norton was found locked in his room with his passkey in his pocket. No one could have entered his room.

When Hastings reports these happenings, Poirot very decidedly says, "Norton did not shoot himself. He was deliberately killed." The next day, Poirot dies from natural causes. He had another one of his small heart attacks—but this time, he didn't have tablets by his bedside.

Hastings is bereft. Not only has he lost his best friend in the world; Poirot left this life with his last case unsolved. In the duel between X and Poirot, it seems that X has won.

One murder attempt (Daisy) and three successful murders (Barbara, Norton, and Poirot) under his/her belt. Who could the scoundrel be?

Poirot leaves a couple clues for Hastings—a directive to go talk to his old valet, and a copy of Shakespeare's *Othello*. Hastings discovers that Poirot had dismissed his longtime valet before he made the trip to Styles. In his place, he hired Curtiss, a hulking, dim-witted man—capable of lifting Poirot up

and down the stairs, but not one
to ask many questions. Why would
Poirot have hired him?

Four months after Poirot's
demise, Hastings gets a posthumous
letter from his friend, explaining
everything: When Poirot had presented those cases to Hastings, he
never said X was the murderer—
just that he had *caused* the murders.
But just as Iago never actually
killed Desdemona in Shakespeare's
famous play, he was certainly culpa-

ble. Iago had worked his evil spell of suggestion to drive Othello to murder his own wife! X used the same technique. X knew just what buttons to push to goad the nicest, seemingly innocent people to kill. After all, didn't it even happen to Hastings? Luckily, Poirot was clever enough to drug Hastings' cocoa so that he could be stopped.

It was Norton—the meek, mild bird enthusiast—who was X. He pushed Colonel Luttrell's buttons to make him shoot his wife. At first, he had tried his power of suggestion on Dr. Franklin. Franklin's clinical mind wasn't susceptible, but his wife's was! Through Norton's seemingly innocuous hints, she came to see how her husband was such a disappointment to her. Because of him she had missed her chance with Boyd Carrington— and wouldn't it be better if her husband were out of the way? So she played up the notion that

Franklin may be experimenting on himself with certain drugs, all in the name of science. She put the drug in his coffee that night. But Hastings had turned around the revolving bookcase, and the coffees were switched. Hastings had inadvertently killed Barbara! Poirot protected him by saying that Barbara had been suicidal.

Most shockingly, it was Poirot who "executed" Norton. It had to be done—who knew how many more victims he would prey upon? At his hand, at least eight persons had either attempted or succeeded in committing murder—and it was clear to Poirot that Norton meant to pin Barbara's murder on Judith (through his seemingly innocuous hints, of course). How many lives was he going to ruin? Poirot knew there was no other way—Norton had to be stopped.

Throughout the whole stay, Poirot was pretending to be a bit more feeble than he really was. Though very sick, he was still very mobile. The night that Norton visited him, Poirot revealed what he knew, and coolly told Norton that he intended to kill him. Norton seemed amused. Undeterred, Poirot put tranquilizer in Norton's drink, then laid the sleeping Norton in his bed, shot him square between the eyes, and planted the passkey on Norton's body. Poirot (having made another passkey) dressed in his victim's colorful bathrobe and walked the hall, posing as Norton. That was who Hastings had seen!

Once Poirot did his duty, he knew it was time for his final rest. He decided not to have his pills by his bedside anymore, and drifted off to his death. He leaves Hastings with the best wishes for his daughter (he knows that she and Dr. Franklin will be very happy together, going to Africa for their research). And he suggests that

Miss Cole may be a good match for Hastings.

With this last act, Poirot has taken his final bow—a brilliant curtain call for a brilliant career.

Agatha Christie: A Brief Biography

*"I regard my work as
no importance—
I've simply been out to entertain."*

—Agatha Christie

Agatha Mary Clarissa Miller was born in 1890 in Torquay, England, and grew up on the estate of Ashfield in a happy, well-to-do home. When she was eleven, her father died, and the family found themselves in reduced circumstances. Yet Agatha was still able to go to a Paris finishing school, and later made a trip to Cairo with her mother, which began a lifetime love of Middle East travels.

AGATHA CHRISTIE, 1924

Her first attempt at writing was inspired by a bout with the flu, when she found herself bored in bed. Her mother asked, "Why don't you write a story? . . . You don't know that you can't, because you've never tried." She produced a novella called *Snow Upon the Desert*, which she sent to an editor to get his keen advice on how to improve her writing.

In the meantime, World War I began, and in 1914 she married the dashing Royal pilot Archibald Christie. Like many women during the war, she volunteered as a nurse and then at the dispensary, which gave her much access and knowledge of various poisons. It was while working with these medicines that she hatched her first idea for a real detective story, which later became *The Mysterious Affair at Styles*, featuring Hercule Poirot. It was published in 1920, and thus began a writing career that would span a half-century.

In 1926, around the time that one of her most successful novels, *The Murder of Roger Ackroyd*, was winning acclaim, Archie asked for a divorce, saying that he had fallen in love with another woman. That same year, Agatha's mother died, which launched her into a nervous breakdown and resulted in her much-publicized disappearance for eleven days.

But Agatha soon rallied: In 1928, as a thirty-eight-year-old divorcee, and mother to the nine-year-old Rosalind, she randomly canceled a trip to the West Indies in favor of visiting Baghdad. She took the Orient Express, a train that ran from London to Istanbul, which soon became the inspiration for one of her most famous mysteries, *Murder on the Orient Express*. Upon her second trip to the Middle East the following year, she met the young archaeologist Max Mallowan, who was fourteen years her junior. They married in 1930 and embarked on a happy union that would last almost fifty years.

Not only was she now a famous mystery writer, Agatha Christie Mallowan was also the wife of a renowned archaeologist. She accompanied Max on many of his digs in far-flung places like Ur, Basra, and Iraq, and some of her mysteries reflect her fascination with this part of the world, including *Death on the Nile* and *Death Comes as the End* (a mystery set in Ancient Egypt). She also wrote an account of her experience on the digs, called *Come, Tell Me How You Live*.

Whether she was in England or on a far-away expedition, she continued to write at least one detective story every year, and even wrote romances under the pseudonym Mary Westacott. But it was mainly the "whodunits," with those brilliant twist endings, that won her acclaim. In addition to her Hercule

Poirot and Miss Marple mysteries, some of her most famous stories are *Ten Little Indians (And Then There Were None)* and *Witness for the Prosecution*, as well as the longest-running play in history, *The Mousetrap*.

Christie became a Dame of the British Empire in 1971, just three years after Max was knighted for his contributions to archaeology. She died in January 1976.

Complete List of Poirot Mysteries

❧

The Mysterious Affair at Styles, 1920

The Murder on the Links, 1923

Poirot Investigates, 1924 *(short stories)*

The Murder of Roger Ackroyd, 1926

The Big Four, 1927

The Mystery of the Blue Train, 1928

Peril at End House, 1932

Lord Edgware Dies, 1933

Murder on the Orient Express, 1934

Three Act Tragedy, 1935

Death in the Clouds, 1935

The ABC Murders, 1936

Murder in Mesopotamia, 1936

Cards on the Table, 1936

Murder in the Mews, 1937

Dumb Witness, 1937

Death on the Nile, 1937

Appointment with Death, 1938

art credits

❖❖❖

This book has been bound using
handcraft methods and Smyth-sewn
to ensure durability.

Designed by Susan Van Horn.

Written by Jennifer Kasius.

Edited by Cindy De La Hoz.

The text was set in Edwardian, Bembo,
ITC Kabel, and Futura.